PENGUIN B(
SELECTED POEMS

JIBANANANDA DAS, one of the greatest poets of the subcontinent, was born in 1899, received a master's degree in English from the University of Calcutta and taught in a number of colleges including City College, Calcutta, Ramjas College, Delhi, and B.M. College, Barisal. His first volume of poetry was *Jhara Palak* (Fallen Feathers, 1927) while his best-known collections include *Banalata Sen* (1942) and *Rupasi Bangla* (Beautiful Bengal, written in 1934 and published in 1957). Though principally a poet, Jibanananda also wrote essays, short stories and novels. While his early poems evoke the rural and natural beauty of Bengal, his later poems reflect the depression, frustration and loneliness of urban life. His stories and novels analyse the complexities of marital life and sexual relationships as well as the society and politics of his time.

Jibanananda died in a tram accident in Calcutta in 1954.

*

CHIDANANDA DAS GUPTA was born in 1921. Leading film critic and film-maker, he founded the Calcutta Film Society with Satyajit Ray in 1947. Chidananda is also well known for his translations of Rabindranath Tagore, Manik Bandopadhyay and Jibanananda Das. His close association with Jibanananda during the poet's lifetime gives him unique insights into various aspects of the poet's work. Chidananda is the author of *Talking about Films*, *The Painted Face: Studies in India's Popular Cinema* and *The Cinema of Satyajit Ray*. He has edited *Satyajit Ray: An Anthology of Statements on Ray and by Ray* and translated a volume of Jibanananda Das's poetry with an introduction, *Jibanananda Das*, as part of the Makers of Indian Literature series for Sahitya Akademi.

Chidananda Das Gupta lives and works in Calcutta and Santiniketan.

Selected Poems

JIBANANANDA DAS

*Translated from the Bengali
with an introduction by*
CHIDANANDA DAS GUPTA

PENGUIN BOOKS

PENGUIN BOOKS
Published by the Penguin Group
Penguin Books India Pvt. Ltd, 11 Community Centre, Panchsheel Park, New Delhi 110 017, India
Penguin Group (USA) Inc., 375 Hudson Street, New York, NewYork 10014, USA
Penguin Group (Canada), 90 Eglinton Avenue East, Suite 700, Toronto, M4P 2Y3 (a division of Pearson Penguin Canada Inc.)
Penguin Books Ltd, 80 Strand, London WC2R 0RL, England
Penguin Ireland, 25 St Stephen's Green, Dublin 2, Ireland (a division of Penguin Books Ltd)
Penguin Group (Australia), 250 Camberwell Road, Camberwell, Victoria 3124, Australia (a division of Pearson Australia Group Pty Ltd)
Penguin Group (NZ), cnr Airborne and Rosedale Roads, Albany, Auckland 1310, New Zealand (a division of Pearson New Zealand Ltd)
Penguin Group (South Africa) (Pty) Ltd, 24 Sturdee Avenue, Rosebank, Johannesburg 2196, South Africa

Penguin Books Ltd, Registered Offices: 80 Strand, London WC2R 0RL, England

First published by Penguin Books India 2006
Copyright © Amitananda Das 2006
Translation and introduction copyright © Chidananda Das Gupta 2006

All rights reserved
10 9 8 7 6 5 4 3 2 1

ISBN-13: 978-0-14310-026-3   ISBN-10: 0-14310-026-2

Typeset in Perpetua by Mantra Virtual Services, New Delhi
Printed at Sanat Printers, Kundli, Haryana

This book is sold subject to the condition that it shall not, by way of trade or otherwise, be lent, resold, hired out, or otherwise circulated without the publisher's prior written consent in any form of binding or cover other than that in which it is published and without a similar condition including this condition being imposed on the subsequent purchaser and without limiting the rights under copyright reserved above, no part of this publication may be reproduced, stored in or introduced into a retrieval system, or transmitted in any form or by any means (electronic, mechanical, photocopying, recording or otherwise), without the prior written permission of both the copyright owner and the above-mentioned publisher of this book.

CONTENTS

Introduction vii

Banalata Sen of Natore	1
The Orange	2
The Professor	3
The Lighter Moment	4
Spring Has Passed	6
Bombers at Dawn, 1942	7
Spectral	8
Leaning against the Sky	9
Wasted Moments	10
Name Me a Word	11
Voices in a Dream	12
Twenty Years Hence	13
Darkness	15
A Moment	17
A Strange Darkness	18
Tonight	19
Icy Winds	20
The Deer	21
Days and Nights	22
Human Tales	23
Why Do the Stars	24
Near and Far	25
The Signet	26
Evening Comes	30
The Moon atop the Field	31

These Days and Nights	32
City	36
Poetry	37
Loving You I Learn	38
The Seagull	40
The Night	43
Within My Head	45
The Vultures	48
Suchetana	49
The Streets of Babylon	51
The Corpse	52
The Cat	53
One Day Eight Years Ago	54
The Windy Night	57
Wild Swans	59
The Aeons, Like Fireflies	60
Winter Night	61
Into These Ears	62
Nine Swans	63
In the Likeness of the Sun	64
Epitaph	66
The Traveller	67
Anupam Tribedi	69
The Harvest Is Over	70
Rainy Night	71
The Smell of Far Worlds	73
What Else, Before Death?	74
I Will Leave It All	76
Starlight	77
Three Stray Stanzas	79
To You	80
Mortal Swans	81
Death at the Turn of the Century	82

INTRODUCTION

The Tagore umbrella so overshadowed the entire arena of Bengali culture for upwards of half a century that it is hardly possible to introduce the poetry of Jibanananda Das (1899–1954) without referring to Tagore.

Rabindranath Tagore (1861–1941), poet, novelist, philosopher, painter, music composer, educationist, was an altogether formidable figure of his times. An innate faith in non-violence, in the synthesis of East and West, tradition and modernity, a broad, liberal humanism and social reformism provided the underpinnings of his outlook. A nobility of spirit pervaded his writings, pronouncements and actions, and overawed generations in India. The Nobel Prize gave him an exalted place in the international firmament.

No wonder in his salad days the young Jibanananda would send his poems to Rabindranath Tagore, hoping for words of encouragement, only to be met with an embarrassed disapproval. To Tagore, elegance of language was as vital as richness of meaning, striking roots in tradition as important as being contemporary. Perhaps he could not stomach the young aspirant's lines like 'From the spittle, the blood and the excreta/the fly rises into the sunlight' or 'Turning the hydrant on... The leper licks up water'. The patriarch admitted that the young poet had some talent but complained that he persecuted the language. It seems eminently possible that thoughts and images in a poem like 'One Day Eight Years Ago', with its contemplations on the corpse of a man lying in the morgue, who has killed himself for no apparent reason, would cause the old poet some discomfort:

> Was this the sleep of his longing—
> The sleep of the plague rat, foaming blood at the mouth
> Neck thrust into the dark crevice,
> Never to wake again?
>
> 'Never to awake, never to know
> The unbearable burden of knowing,
> And knowing always, never'—
> Said to him, after the moon had set,
> A silence, creeping up to his window,
> Like a camel's neck.

Yet, Tagore often had thoughts on who his successor might one day be:

> I wake up on this autumnal dawn and wonder
> O my bamboo flute, to whom shall I hand you over
> Now that it is time for me to go?

Clearly, Jibanananda was not the one he had in mind. Little did he think that the young man would one day emerge as Bengal's most important poet of the post-Tagore era, destined to bring into Bengali poetry of his times an anguished awareness of modernity, in striking language and imagery.

Yet, Jibanananda's reverence for Tagore ran very deep, as his many odes to the old poet and numerous prose writings show. Jibanananda had no time for groups of modern poets who were, somewhat self-consciously, trying to disentangle themselves from the thousand threads that bound them to Tagore as the pivot round which they revolved.

During the 1930s, the search for liberation from Tagore became a deliberate pursuit with a whole generation of poets, among whom Buddhadev Bose was perhaps the most articulate. For some fifteen years before Tagore's death, the Kallol group, centring round the magazine of the same name and consisting of individuals strongly influenced by either English poetry of post-war frustration or the Marxist utopia or both, sought paths for the expression of a post-war sensibility. And Kallol was by no means the only force that ranged itself in the struggle for freedom from Tagorean values and stylistics. As Bishnu Dey declared in a poem written on Tagore's birthday:

> No merchandising of Tagore, any more.
> For us no tying up of the primal river
> In hairy knots of permanence; We keep open
> The Ganga of our souls,
> Reach out to the sea in songs.
> In new line and colour, picture and poem
> We open up joyous new streams.

Not only did Jibanananda not begin by revolting against Tagore, but the development of his spirit paralleled the evolution of Tagore more than of any other post-Tagore poet. Of this he must have been intensely aware himself, for he wrote:

> Poets are not born as a result of a conspiracy to overthrow the great poets preceding them... With the exception of a few poems by one or two poets, the ephemeral stamp on the rest of modern Bengali poetry is so marked that a moment's encounter with a song or poem of Tagore makes us grateful for his vast difference from them... *It is with the help of pointers from Tagore that modern Bengali poetry has made a tiny start* [emphasis mine], and its development will not culminate in the demolition of the fundamentals of Bengali literature or of Tagore...

Jibanananda's strength lay in the way he carried the Tagore legacy forward into the spirit and the idiom of a new era, rather than stand in opposition to it. Indeed, he provides a perfect example of the relationship of tradition and individual talent so precisely articulated by T.S. Eliot in his seminal essay on the subject.

It was a period of Bengali literature buffeted by winds from the West, blowing across the wasteland lying between the two world wars. The moral certitudes of the Victorian era had collapsed, science on the threshold of the nuclear age had bred new uncertainties of its own, and Marxism had raised the red flag in many corners of the devastated landscape.

Significantly, most of the creators of modern Bengali poetry in the late-Tagore period were professors of English literature—Buddhadev Bose, Bishnu Dey, Amiya Chakravarty, Samar Sen, Jibanananda Das. If they were not actually teachers, they were otherwise immersed in the deployment of the language. Quite often, the deeper a poet's knowledge of English literature, the more vigorous and individual his particular synthesis of East and West would be. For instance, Sudhindranath Datta, one of the creators of contemporary Bengali prose, blended a sophisticated knowledge of Sanskrit literature with the cultivation of European classical and contemporary literatures, to write modern Bengali poetry.

But one factor separates Jibanananda from these contemporaries—they were, for the most part, bred in the city; the major influence on Jibanananda's upbringing was the rural ambience. In this respect, he was closer to the novelist Bibhutibhusan Bandopadhyay, known outside Bengal as the writer of *Pather Panchali* and *Aparajita*, on which Satyajit Ray based his famous cinematic trilogy. The poem 'What Else, Before Death?', among others, bears vivid witness to this:

> We who have walked the fields of hay in the autumn twilight
> Seen the dim women at the river sprinkling flowers of fog;
> Women of the dim past, of distant villages;
> We who have seen the trees filled with fireflies,
> Seen the unavaricious moon stand at the top of the field without
>
> crop;

Jibanananda had no awareness of 'the beautiful' or 'the poetic' and did not build up his own conventions around them; the ugly is made vivid and meaningful by the force of his vision. Alongside nature, the animal world has its own part (rather as in Edith Sitwell), sometimes in the most 'unpoetic' forms—the sores on the dying horse, the doddering old owl, the vulture, the circus lion, the frog, the mosquito. Flowers are relatively rare, but plants and trees are present very specifically, with their names spelt out. Sometimes the use is so literal as to be startling—as in the comparison of someone's eyes with the cane fruit. City dwellers may not know that the cane fruit looks very like the human eye.

But the city also formed a major strand of the poet's awareness emanating from his long, often unhappy, encounter with Calcutta. There he studied English literature at Presidency College and took his master's degree from Calcutta University. Thereafter he taught English for some time at City College, Calcutta, an institution founded by Brahmos, who, as legend has it, dismissed him for having referred to the glories of the female bosom in one of his poems. After moving from one college to another in Delhi and Dhaka, he returned to his native town of Barisal to teach English literature at Brajamohan College there. But this was not destined to last long; when, with the partition of India, East Bengal became East Pakistan, he chose to stay on in Calcutta where he had gone on a visit. The intermittent nature of his employment as a lecturer and long bouts of unemployment meant constant financial stringency. One might also doubt how congenial he found it to conform to college schedules and examination syllabi. He is known to have been under considerable pressure from the family to find substantial employment instead of wasting his time on poetry that they, like the generality of readers of the time, found too obscure. He tried his hand at many different jobs but none of them suited his highly introspective temperament. Success eluded him all his life.

It was only after Tagore's death in 1941 and his own in 1954 that Jibanananda Das began to attract significant attention. Soon thereafter, he emerged as the foremost Bengali poet whose many volumes of poetry came into widespread demand.

*

A.K. Ramanujan, the Kannada poet, linguist and translator, once commented that Bengali poetry was obsessed with transcendence. Had he come across Ramanujan's comment, Jibanananda might have countered by asking of what use poetry would be if it was not concerned with transcendence, a prime element of Jibanananda Das's value-world. The moral imperative is brought to bear on all the world's goings-on, no matter how elevated or lowly; the flux of the world always contains within it the possibility of ascending to a higher moral order. And this is a matter of human choice; it is not deterministic, unlike the socialist vision. Despite his shortcomings, man is destined to fulfil his possibilities. To him, as to Tagore, it is a sin to lose faith in the human being, in spite of occasional despair:

> I have striven, worn my feet roving.
> Seeking to give man what belongs to him,
> And I am weary roving in the burning sun of day.
> Yet so trying to love man,
>
> I see man, my own flesh and blood,
> Strewn around dead, killed by my own hand.
> The world is sick and in pain
> Yet we are its debtors, and shall remain.
>
> —'Suchetana'

But elsewhere:

> Come then, let us to ourselves and to our own worlds
> Determine to shine in total truth.
> Is time marching towards a new dawn?
> O quarters of the earth, somewhere I hear the bird,
> Somewhere there is sunrise yet to be met.
>
> —'In the Likeness of the Sun'

The word 'yet' is one of the most frequently used in Jibanananda's vocabulary. It provides the nexus between his agony over the present human condition and his faith in man's deliverance from it. Sometimes, especially in his early poetry, the agony is too much to bear. Man, weary with the blows history has dealt him, wants to go back to where he came from, embracing death, and the darkness of the womb. The cry of pain is loud and uninhibited, and the death wish is unashamed:

> With fear and pain I saw
> The red sun ordering me to stand to attention,
> My face turned stiffly towards the world.
> My heart filled with hatred
> For the world fermented in the heat of the sun,
> Festive with the squealing of pigs,
> Bursting with sordid joy.
>
> Drowning that roaring sun
> In the unrelenting darkness of my heart,
> I sought to go to sleep again,
> To merge into the breast of the dark,
> Into the vaginal darkness of limitless death.
>
> —'Darkness'

*

Jibanananda (*Jiban* = life, *Ananda* = joy; Jibanananda, one who delights in life) was born to a Brahmo family in the small town of Barisal, now in Bangladesh. The Brahmos formed a modern Hindu sect committed to religious and social reform with monotheistic beliefs derived from the later Vedic texts known as the Upanishads. In social reform their emphasis was on democracy and women's rights. Jibanananda's father, Satyananda, was a noted schoolteacher and his mother a recognized poet. The name they gave to their eldest son is not common among

Bengalis; indeed, the suffix 'ananda' is usually given to one at the time of joining a Hindu renunciate order as in the cases of Swami Vivekananda, Swami Prajnananda etc. Among the laity, giving such a name would indicate a spiritual bent of mind in the parents not unusual among Brahmos of the time.

Jibanananda had little interest in the ritualistic aspects of religion, but spirituality as an ally of introspection was undoubtedly close to his nature. His sensuous response to nature too had a contemplative, spiritual dimension to it:

> The good earth called me to be born
> In human home, and I,
> Knowing I should not, yet came.
> The meaning of this I know now;
> For with the tip of my finger
> I have touched the stuff
> Of the dew on the leaf at dawn.
>
> —'Suchetana'

The mainly rural surroundings of Barisal, with its openness to nature, its fields and rivers, animals and birds, left a deep impress on the poet that stayed with him all his life and coloured his poetry. From his childhood ambience, Jibanananda must have imbibed an abiding interest in nature, an inwardness of the spirit and a sense of the moral imperative, all of them plentifully evident in his poems.

*

The originality of his imagery is perhaps the most striking aspect of the poetry of Jibanananda Das. In writing about him in a language other than his own, it is the best starting point in studying him because, even in translation, something of the power of the images comes through. Many of the images involve a transposition of sense categories:

> As the footfall of dew comes evening;
> The raven wipes the smell of warm sun
> From its wings;
>
> —'Banalata Sen'

The imagery is relatively free from Sanskritic conventions; it is drawn more from rural experience, from unusual modes of expression, from history, geographical specifics and the vocabulary of science, rather than from mythology or the Vaisnavite or Saivite cults. The images are culled from a wide range of rural and urban experience as also across vast distances in time and space, historical and geographical landmarks. Vidisha and Sravasti, Babylon and Attila, Patanjali and Nagarjuna jostle each other, brought together by a rapidly connecting imagination. In the subtitle to a poem, 'The Last Night of Capricorn', he compares the consciousness of the historical flow of time to the flight of a bird. At times the image is taken so directly from English usage, as in 'The Epitaph', that the meaning in the original leaps out only in translation:

> Here lies Sarojini; (I do not know
> If she still lies here); she has lain here for long;

In the Bengali original, the first line does not at once suggest a grave; it is almost as though the poet is referring to a woman lying in bed; then, at the end of the second line, you guess the Englishness of the phrase, used in Bengali so unexpectedly. It makes the transcendence more striking when, at the end, we read:

> A dry saffron light lingers in the sky
> Like an invisible cat
> On whose face sits an obstreperous smile
> Of hollow cunning.

Sometimes the images are photographic, even cinematic:

> The shadow of the thatched roof is etched in the moonlit yard

Or

> The unflickering light, there, where the lovely maidens
> of the world glide into bodies of incense

The individual images are then lifted on to a transcendental plane:

> What else need we know before death? Do we not know
> How at the edge of each red desire rises like a wall
> The grey face of death? The dreams and the gold of the earth
> Reach a tranquil equilibrium, ending a magic need.
> What else need we know?
> Have we not heard the cries of birds upon the dying sun?
> Have we not seen the crow fly across the mist?

*

A far cry from all this is 'A Lighter Moment', very urbane, ironical, even bitter, but deeply in empathy with the object of irony. The three beggars and the destitute woman who joins them at their evening get-together declare their disdain of wealth, and their proud independence:

> These frothy words rouse the ire of a mosquito
> That leaps from the tip of one nose to another,
> As by the river of Bentinck Street they sit
> Counting on their fingers the goods of the world

The ironical strand yields suddenly to transcendence:

> For now they will depart for the land of the flying river
> Where the bedevilled monkey and the broken bone
> Come together to the edge of the water

And reflect upon the reflections
As long as there is time to reflect.

Jibanananda is happier with specifics than with species. Rivers, animals, birds are mostly named; rivers like Kirtinasha and the Dhansiri, birds like the bulbul and the khanjana, trees like the hijal and the ashwattha, and so on. His men and women have names and surnames—Arunima Sanyal, whose face evokes rural Bengal; Mrinalini Ghosal, whose corpse lies in its watery grave amidst the red and blue fish; Shephalika Bose, whose laughter is heard from behind the forest of hijal trees in moonlight. In his most famous single poem, Jibanananda gives us a place name too—Banalata Sen of Natore. The men too have names and surnames—Anupam Tribedi, Subinoy Mustafi and so on. The women are *sympathique*, the men smart, successful, perhaps too smart to escape a shade of ridicule:

> Anupam Tribedi's face fades in on this cold night,
> Although he is no longer physically tumbling
> Inside the belly of the rotund earth.
> The silence of winter standing at the table
> Brings his memory bustling back into the thoughts
> Of the dead and the living; the books on the table
> Bend the mind to all from Plato to Tagore
> Who, after emptying their thoughts on us,
> Sleep now under dewy blankets out in the cold.
> Tribedi, having snuffed out his candle on earth,
> Must be waking them from their slumber.
> —'Anupam Tribedi'

In the directions of his strength, Jibanananda goes far beyond his contemporaries in Bengal. In him we have a sensuous, rustic poet with a profound feeling for the rural environment; an urbane, very contemporary mind shuttling across a wide range of time and space; a regional poet without provinciality, concerned with human destiny; a thinking man with an ability to state philosophical thought in exciting poetry, aware of tradition yet free of the cobwebs of convention. It is a formidable range to assay with the intensity that became his hallmark.

Jibanananda never lived outside poetry. He did write some short stories and novels with distinction, but it was poetry that filled his being. In him there was no Tagorean unity in the art of writing and the art of living, between the life of the imagination and life lived in the politico-social environment—either in Barisal, where he spent his youth, or in Calcutta, where he lived his later years. His mind was withdrawn from the immediacy of life around him, yet he keenly observed it—from a distance. His living participation in it was solely through his work. 'If he is really a poet,' he himself said in an essay, 'it will not be possible for him to offer to the world of the daily grind a second gift as extraordinary as the first, which is his poetry.'

Sad as it was, it was not without some poetic justice that such a man lost his life by being run over by a passing tramcar.

Even before his death, bathos haunted his life. People often took him for the very opposite of what he was—an intensely alive and warm-hearted human being. For a long time, he was the butt-end of ridicule not only by conventionalists like Sajanikanto Das who gleefully attacked him in almost every issue of the weekly magazine *Sanibarer Chithi* (The Saturday Letter) but also by many who laid claims to modernity. Legend has it that some members of his family surrounded him once and demanded to know who this Banalata Sen was and why he, a married man, was carrying on with her. Whether the story is apocryphal or not, it illustrates issues germane to his times and to him. In daily life, he wore a mask of stony intractability that few could penetrate to get through to the man. Certainly, his was a life far removed from the Tagorean model of tranquil unity and comprehensive synthesis. It was much more typical of the contemporary period with its tensions, its secret core of pain, its disbelief and disillusion.

Jibanananda was not only a poet; he was nothing but a poet.

September 2006   Chidananda Das Gupta

Banalata Sen of Natore

For aeons have I roamed the roads of the earth
From the seas of Ceylon to the straits of Malaya
I have journeyed, alone, in the enduring night,
And down the dark corridor of time I have walked
Through mist of Bimbisara, Asoka, darker Vidarbha.
Round my weary soul the angry waves still roar;
My only peace I knew with Banalata Sen of Natore.

Her hair was dark as night in Vidisha;
Her face the sculpture of Sravasti.
I saw her, as a sailor after the storm
Rudderless in the sea, spies of a sudden
The grass-green heart of the leafy island.
'Where were you so long?' she asked, and more
With her bird's-nest eyes, Banalata Sen of Natore.

As the footfall of dew comes evening;
The raven wipes the smell of warm sun
From its wings; the world's noises die.
And in the light of fireflies the manuscript
Prepares to weave the fables of night;
Every bird is home, every river reached the ocean.
Darkness remains; and time for Banalata Sen.

'Banalata Sen', *Banalata Sen*

The Orange

Once I am dead,
Shall I ever come back to earth again?

If so be it that I do,
Let me come back, on a wintry night,
As the frail, cold flesh of a half-eaten orange
Set on a table, by the dying one's bed.

'Kamlalebu', *Banalata Sen*

The Professor

With a wan smile I said:
'Why do you not with your own hand
Pen the poem?'—The shadow made no reply.
And small wonder, for he was no poet,
But only the timeless Prologue
Seated on a gilded throne
Of ink, Mss, and notes of his own.

No, no poet, only a toothless professor
Seeking eternity, drawing fifteen hundred a month
For picking to the bone fifteen hundred poets
Once living, but now altogether dead,
Scattering the flesh and the wriggling worms
To the four winds; though once they had sought
To warm their hands at the fire of life,
Felt pangs of hunger and of love,
And swum with the sharks on the seas.

'Samarudha', *Saat-ti Tarar Timir*

The Lighter Moment

Now at the end of day
The three not quite virginal beggars
Find their minds attuning to the quiet.
Swallowing a mouthful of air
They stand over the roadside
And with another mouthful of air
Rinse their precious mouths.
For now they are bound for the land of the red river,
Where the washerman and his donkey
Ride magically on each other's back
And reflect upon the reflections in the water.

Yet before they depart, the three beggars get together
Sit in a circle around three mugs of tea,
One styling himself king, the other king's minister
The third, his august general.
A beggar woman too, out of sheer love
Of her three lame uncles
Or getting related precipitately
By no more than the lure of tea, draws near,
And four pairs of mouths and ears melt together
In one infernal harmony.

They pour some water from the hydrant
Into the tea, seeking to make life
More honest, more full of sympathy.
One shook his head and said:
'What good would be the well-filtered water
Of Chetla's market or the spouts of Tala
Since neither a husband's brother nor a brother's wife

Would spare a copper for the beggar?'
Thus they pronounced, shaking their shaggy manes
As they cast their eye on the lone woman,
Feeling her presence as a ghost of a female,
Caught there amidst them in the dim steam of a cup of tea;
Perhaps once a swan, now no more than a lame duck.
She had a cup, yet they came out with another one.
'We have no gold, yet we are slaves of none.'
These frothy words rouse the ire of a mosquito
That leaps from the tip of one nose to another,
As by the river of Bentinck Street they sit
Counting on their fingers the goods of the world,
Stroking their hair into angry buns they counted
The why and wherefore of all expenditure;
To whom are payments made, to what end
And by whom, at what hour of dusk,
And how retribution overtakes the wary, calculating devils.
Speculation was rife on what would happen
If to a man one gave
The life-giving medicine, free of cost,
After he was altogether dead.
For now they will depart for the land of the flying river
Where the bedevilled monkey and the broken bone
Come together to the edge of the water
And reflect upon the reflections
As long as there is time to reflect.

'Laghu muhurta', *Saat-ti Tarar Timir*

Spring Has Passed

At close of day the immemorial foxes
Enter in quest of kill the hill-side forest,
And prowling in silence in the inviolate dark,
Come upon a clearing, and suddenly behold—

The snow sleeping in moonlight.
Could their quadruped beings cry out upon the moment,
As with human souls, the event of their heart,
Then would a wonder deep as pain dawn
In their minds;—So in the dark of the blood
My soul leaps up when you appear,
Suddenly, after spring has passed.

'Shei sab sheyalera', *Saat-ti Tarar Timir*

Bombers at Dawn, 1942

Somewhere I see a few birds
And dew drying in the sun.
In their paddy fields a few men,
Solitary as mankind, stand.
And the ripples on the earth
Pining for some divine geometry
Merge into the skies of the past
And of today.

Is the horizon on strike?
A lone chimney has spread itself
Like a bird across the blue.
Reflected in the river's water
Clear as the eyes of the crow,
Clouds climb into the sky
Like winding stairs
In soulful fusion with nature.

The glory of fission descends;
I smell alum in the sky
And count the planes.
Pretending to watch the azure,
I stare at the ghost of the century
Lit up by the sun.

'Bhor o chhoyti bomar', Agranthita Kavita

Spectral

Lying at the edge of a cloud
On this night full of stars,
What am I—a spectre or a soul?

I take one look at the solitary, moonlit sea
Over which ashes fly like sand for miles.
At its end stands a behemoth
Surveying proudly his playground.

I raise my eyes and fly from one star to another
Silenced by the ignorance of the heart.

Of an autumn night
A pack of foxes go hunting rabbits
And, suddenly, assailed by human sense,
Tremble in their bones
At the spectral presence
Of moon and forest,
So alike.

'Danabiya', Agranthita Kavita

Leaning against the Sky

Don't go there, Suranjana
Don't talk to that young man.
Come back to the night of silvery stars,
Come back to these fields, waves;
Come back to my heart.

Don't go far, farther, farther away
With that young man;
What do you want with him, him?

In the sky beyond the skies
You are as earth today
And his love as the straw flying on it.

Suranjana, your heart is as straw today;
Breeze flies across breeze
Skies lie beyond the sky.

'Akashleena', *Saat-ti Tarar Timir*

Wasted Moments

Having wasted myriad moments
I now know time is eternity
But love is not all about that.

Yet, having loved you
And then returned to myself,
I have learnt that my heart
Remains awake wherever I station it—
In time told by the clock
Or in time eternal.

'Anek muhurta aami', Agranthita Kavita

Name Me a Word

Name me a word
Great, simple, vast as the sky
A word that has, like the intimate hand
Of the woman I have loved forever,
Washed the dirty innards of history
And all its tired, wounded and dead
In blood; blood of the ones fed on
Food left out for hungry animals.

Like that starlit night stirred by the wind
Like that day agog with engine-driven wings
Of the bird that sees all the thirst of all birds
As the last pure flame of the dying candle.

'Amake ekti katha dao', *Bela Abela Kalbela*

Voices in a Dream

Whispers came up within my dream and said
Senility is best, it's the ultimate.
Into my inert eyes
Enters the light of another noon.
Forsaking the arabesques of golden thread in the sky
I lie in the dark
Under the sky black with bats' wings
Leaning my back on the wall of dark
Praying for decrepitude to descend upon me.

'Swapner dhwanira', *Banalata Sen*

Twenty Years Hence

If I should meet her again
Twenty years hence
Of an autumn evening
As the crow wings its way home
As the yellow river lies down
Beside the white flowers
Amidst the sheaves of rice;

Or perhaps the rice has fled;
The bustle of harvest over;
Under the bird's nest
The hay has spread itself;
And in the home of the singing bird
The dew and the night's cold condensed;

If I should suddenly see you
Walking down the path amidst the fields.

Perhaps the moon will wink
From behind a filigree of leaves
With fine black twigs of the tamarind tree
Across its face.

If I should see you again,
Twenty years hence
When your memory has faded,
Perhaps the owl
Will crawl down to the field
Hide itself in the lanes
And windows of the trees

Silent as the eyelid coming down over the eye
Golden kites descend.
The owl is claimed by the dawn.

What if I should find you again
Across twenty years of a misty curtain?

       'Kudi bachhar parey', *Banalata Sen*

Darkness

I woke up to the sounds of the river
Lapping upon the shore.
The pale moon had withdrawn its shade
From one river to another.

In the early winter night I lay
Alongside the river with the terraced rice-fields
Knowing that never, never
Would I awake again.

O you moon, glowing blue as the musk deer
Unlike the enterprise of daylight, yet no dream,
You have no power to stir
The stillness of death that reigns in my heart.
The sleep that envelopes me is too deep
For you to destroy.

Don't you know, blue musk-deer moon,
I woke up to the stupid light of day
And saw myself again as a creature of the earth
And I was afraid.

With fear and pain I saw
The red sun ordering me to stand to attention,
My face turned stiffly towards the world,
My heart filled with hatred
For the world fermented in the heat of the sun,
Festive with the squealing of pigs,
Bursting with sordid joy.

Drowning that roaring sun
In the unrelenting darkness of my heart,
I sought to go to sleep again,
To merge into the breast of the dark,
Into the vaginal darkness of limitless death.

I was never human;
I have not seen you before,
Nor this your world;
Yet I am not of another planet.
Where there is tremor and speed,
Thought and action,
There lie the sun, the earth, Venus
And endless other knots in vast spaces
Echoing to the squealing of pigs
And the groans of countless sows in labour.

My soul is curled up in sleep and darkness;
Why awaken me?
O you knots in the thread of time
You sun, you cuckoo of the winter night
You cold wind of memory
Why do you labour to awaken me?

I shall not wake up again in the dead of night
To the sound of the river lapping upon the shore;
I shall not see the solitary moon
Withdrawing half its shadow from one river to another.

Upon the terraced side of the water
I shall lie in the early winter night
Knowing that I shall never, never
Awaken again.

'Andhakar', *Banalata Sen*

A Moment

In the moonlit forest
Reigns the smell of the tiger—
My heart is as the flying deer—
Where am I headed
In this silent forest night?

Shadows of silvery leaves
Lie across my body;
The deer have fled.
Wherever I go
A sickle-bent moon
Has sliced out the field's last crop of deer
And is now sinking
Into the congealed darkness of the eyes
Of hundreds of sleeping beings.

'Muhurta', *Mahaprithivi*

A Strange Darkness

In this strange darkness descended upon the day
The finest vision belongs to the blind.
The world is led by the counsel
Of the loveless, pitiless ghosts;
And upon the hearts of those that yet believe
In light, in the undying flame of man's enduring quest
Hyenas and vultures feast.

'Adbhut adhar ek', *Sreshtha Kavita*

Tonight

It would have been nice to have had you here
Tonight; we could have talked, among the trees, under the stars.

But I have found,
Working through the laws that regulate
Thought, feeling and emotion,
That in their end result, in India or China,
New York or London, the mystery of tonight
And the history of mammoths all
Fall into patterns inevitable,
Where are you at this moment,
With what dice rolling in your hand,
Why enquire; all enquiries do not benefit.

Within the mornings noons rivers stars I have known
Lies all that there is to be known.

'Aajker raat', *Bela Abela Kalbela*

Icy Winds

Out there, where icy winds blow
Rattling the doors and windows
With the hounds of the night,
The snow sleeps in the crevices of the stars
And drips all night.

Journeying across the seas,
And rivers and highways,
A lover has arrived in a cold, dingy room.
From here issue winding staircases
Leading to a maze of rooms.
For these, for reasons unknown,
The world has raised a warning finger:
Which steps then would he take
To go to which room?

Having mounted all the stairs
He arrives at the last empty step.
Life, time and the universe
Yield only one meaning:
The way itself is all.

'Bahey himel hawa', Agranthita Kavita

The Deer

Was it in a dream that I saw the deer
Play in the spring night
Amidst the forest of palash trees

The moon laid its hand on the dewy leaves
The wind shook its wings
Sprinkling pearls through the leaves.

In the eyes of the deer
Play the wind and the pearls.

Lighting diamond lamps
Shephalika Bose laughs
From behind the moonlit hijal trees,
In the countless skies of the forest.

Where is Shephalika,
In what grey, vanished planet,
Only the deer in moonlight know.

'Harinera', *Banalata Sen*

Days and Nights

The day was spent in useless endeavours
The night will go in counsels of despair.
Day and night unite in exculpating diurnal sins
Useful only to fuel waste.

Yet the cactus needle is bathed in gentle dew.
Not a bird flies in the sky—
Laden with the wisdom of the day
They have repaired to their nests.

'Din raat', *Sreshtha Kavita*

Human Tales

Human tales come to an end
What remains is this space
This river and its shore
And the flight of birds,
At the top of the tree
The play of orange sunshine.

It seems as though this sunshine
Was at one time a benchmark
In man's becoming less imperfect
With work, with words,
Going from knowledge
To understanding and beyond.
Time, that spent revolutionary,
No longer reveals the truth,
But cools its hot currents to form a new body
Going from peace to greater peace
Leaving some pillars behind,
Journeying to another dawn.

'Yatri', Agranthita Kavita

Why Do the Stars

Why do the stars come my way
Why does the sky come alive in blue
Why does the moon set itself afloat
Like a golden boat behind the banyan branch
Why is the dust filled with the smell of earth
When it is kissed by the dew?
Why do kash flowers come out in droves
Why do khanjana birds dance
And bulbuls and tuntunis fly around in the woods?
If committees are all we need
To prosper in the cities and ports
If grass is only what is trodden underfoot,
If autos are all we need above,
Why does the khanjana dance
Why does the bulbul fly around in the woods?

'Keno michhey', Agranthita Kavita

Near and Far

Near and far,
Towns and homes collapse;
The sound of villages falling down, rises.
Man has lived long on earth;
Yet his shadow on the wall
Seems only to signal
Death, loss and fear.

But for this nothingness
There is little else on the shores of time.
Yet around man's plans,
Failed thoughts, resolves, phantoms,
Rises another world, made gentle
With the sound of multifarious trees.
On this earth, with this love
And this, the heart's signal.

'Prithiviloke', Agranthita Kavita

The Signet

Sometimes I feel life is like a goose
In a miser's home;
Every morning
It lays a golden egg
And leaves it hidden
Under a pile of straws.

That daily wonder
Takes root in the householder's mind;
No longer does he want to see
The goose at the river at noon
Floating away reflected in water
Far and farther away,
Perhaps getting lost in a distorting mirror
By some wicked wizard's trick.

Yet the goose is the asset—
Perhaps the author of the book of yoga knows—
Perhaps the smooth golden egg is its unwilling product.
Looking upward at the sun
It raises its voice and its throat
And floats away in its adventures with water.
Breeze soft as keya flowers
Goes round the goose's upright.
On the lonely way over icy wilderness
It fears nothing, and not seeking to reverse
The meaning of death, flies on.

Yet, lured by the goose's wondrous notes
I have stalked her in dark fields

To find a cluster of
Stars coming towards me.

A decrepit horse chews on grass;
On its neck and legs the bugs circle
Mimicking the sound of dewdrops.
Yet, did this place, this frozen lake
Belong once to the snow-white horse
And will again one day?

On the other side of the planet
New Babylons raise themselves
To the roar of the lions
On its cornices; and will remain?
Or has it by now collapsed in a heap?
Tell me O Orion, O North Star,
Does some boatswain determine the course
Of those that squander their wealth?

On this side, on the shore of the disfigured river
Man is still blue with primordial slime
Having found nothing in the bowels of the earth
Other than blood and grime.

All this will come to an end one day
Or perhaps a tired history's over-sharp measures.
And their self-defeating darkness
Will impose on us a silence
Born of the skills of creation in tiny grass flowers

The conference table belongs at night's end
To the interpreter, and earlier
To the speakers of the state language.
Having learnt these many tongues
The star performers burn in their own heat.

On our palms lifelines burn to this day
Like rows of ghostly faces;
Hair goes grey, weaving
A pale epic of bricks, stars and me.

Like the dwarf clown's longing
For that last heartwarming laugh.
As he dances across the line of fire,
Unable to stand in one place.

Perhaps the blueness of the sky
Isn't as noble as we used to think.
Man arrives on earth seeking to achieve,
Declaims his aims with pomp,
As though all one needs is a rainbow.
Walking down the earth's long and short days
I have myself thought thus many a time.

On such days have I seen fire shed blood.
And when the fire dies down
An equal darkness descends;
The daughters of the dark sing of the blue
And with sunrise the cosmic clown rises
Red in tooth and claw.

In that light the forest lion
Appears the tame beast of the desert;
The roar of the sea sounds like kindly whispers
Of noble creatures though not of human kind.

If in our century those famed fires
Burn again with renewed splendour
With man the soldier and the genius
Nursing the flames as signalled by time

If monkeys, foxes, and vultures laugh
As the new flames leap
Then would the rewrites of the script
Mend at last the distortions of history.

'Parichayak', *Mahaprithivi*

Evening Comes

It is evening. There is quiet everywhere.
Wisp of hay in its mouth, a sparrow flies quietly home;
A bullock cart winds its way down the village path
The courtyards are full of tight piles of golden hay.

All the world's doves
Are cooing among the clumps of hijal trees;
All the world's beauty
Has spread itself on the grass;
All the world's love is in our two hearts;
The sky has spread its peace out among the skies.

'Sandhya hoy', *Rupasi Bangla*

The Moon atop the Field

The moon stares at me.
Around me lie fallow fields;
Cracks in them hold dewdrops.
Bent and sharp as the sickle,
The moon looks on, as it has done
For endless nights.

Says the moon to me:
The harvest is over,
The sickles have gone blunt,
The hay has been gathered,
The fields are empty,
The cracks in the ground are full of dewdrops;
Why do you then stand alone here, looking on?

I reply:
Endless crops have ripened,
Harvests have gone home,
You have grown old as the earth,
The sickle has lost its edge many times,
The cracks in the ground have held dewdrops,
The hay has been wound;
Why do you then stand alone atop
The fallow fields, and look on?

'Mather galpa', *Dhusar Pandulipi*

These Days and Nights

Sometimes I feel
It is better to sink into the dark
Here, where, at the edge of a restless world,
Inhabit astonishing humans;
They have no king, nor any general;
Over their hearts no Chairman rules;
When their bodies wither
No Trade Union Congress holds out hope.

Many a worker lives here
Others too are here who are not quite workers
Having fallen off the middle-class ladder
They are not dead as yet, albeit
Eternally dead time surrounds them;
Their names are not loathsome, being common enough;
When they lose hearth and home, they do not know
Which set of labour laws they should turn to.
Or where to go for cooking oil, water, food itself
Or air to breathe, or open sea.

What do they add up to—
These hospital beds in Belgachhia, or Jorasanko
Jadavpur or Campbell?
I have not had a reply to such a question,
Suddenly asking itself
Through me, on their behalf:
There are beds but not many,
Not enough for all
And perhaps they are not for those
That don't have beds at home

But simply walk past the banyan tree,
Past the cobbler's den
And other darknesses,
Along the tramway tracks
And the footpaths—
Where for them lies the sky?
After the broken bone the hand gropes in hope
Clutching at the sky that is not there.

Their sky is forever the pavement;
At times there is the ambulance.
War-torn troops come back
To an endless sky.

If on his way
Day turns into night and night into day
The way full of footmarks becomes
Devoid of direction,
Crisscrosses the canal
Between one marketplace and another
Driven by vague signals.

The homeless hoboes
And the ones without food
Need a lot of beds, a bit of rest
And before their multifarious deaths
Moments of peace.
There are those too that
Have assigned their all to hospitals,
Want to bring to the dying—
To the lowliest of the lowly—
A modicum of comfort
Or have felt death so deeply in their bones
That they even want
Another, happier, life for all.

Thank them we must
For their utopias.
For after human thought, action, words
Are washed away in a stream of blood
There will remain an infinite glow
That shines anew.

Half-truths of history lap on the shores of time
Yet we love the life given to us,
Know the meaning of life to be
A good life for all.
But that state lies far in the future;
Pushed by hordes of the blind and the maimed
To an elusive end—
For one famine is followed by another
One war ends in the battle cries of the next—
For greed knows no bounds,
There is no desire left other than
Of coitus without desire;
There is no pleasure other than of
Wiping the smile off another's face.
There is no movement
Other than from the given seat
To the highest,
Making heavier the human load
Of falsehood, suffering and sorrow.

Within a night's dreams
I heard once of a leprous woman
Sing a wonderful song
A deaf-mute divinely play the violin,
One with the deodar tree
He has made his home.
Black as night the black cats
That make love to tinsel birds all night long.

Monsoon rain brings down their blood and grime
And in their midst
Dreams unfold with bated breath
Drunken with the whore's tumescent song
The whorehouse turns into purgatory.
Waking up on the morrow, walking,

I too have seen our world from that vantage point
In the light of day.
In the night too, about to devour delicate female flesh;
I have seen us burn in the flames of the age
Reduced to blood and ashes.

Did the Middle Ages witness so much blood?
Can human heart set aside such counting
And cleanse itself before launching on self-reform?
Are human virtues
As pure as the sky's azure?
Can humility, the final end, be as endless as starlight?

'Eisab dinratri', *Sreshtha Kavita*

City

My soul has encountered many a city
Whose brick and mortar,
Whose words, deeds, hopes
And fallen idols with lost eyes,
Have all entered my head
And got cremated there
In the embers of my distaste.

Yet I have seen the sun rise
Above the same cities
At the edge of a massive cloud,
Seen the same sun above the river port
Bearing loads in the heart of an orange cloud
As earnestly as a peasant in love with his land.
I have seen, above the gas lamps and the minarets,
The stars, like phalanxes of wild duck,
Flying towards some southern sea.

'Shahar', *Mahaprithivi*

Poetry

Knowing we have pristine joy
Implanted deep in our bones
We float along the dirty surfaces of time—
Or else all would be drained out.

And you sky, you were once
The flow of the dawn's stream
But now belong to the frozen seas on
Polar nights. Hence, neither the morning bird
Nor the dusky insect misreads the path of light.

The beggar, with female monkey
—Or lone goat—in tow,
Finds the answer to his question
In the still water held in his palm.

The bat sails out into the dark,
The eternity of the field asserts its power
Over the persistent rise of provincial grass;
The worn brick of the age-old grave
Discovers
The passion of the golden-eyed crickets for each other
As they lie amidst the unwanted reeds;

O sky
Once you were as the silent, frozen sea
Of the polar night
Now but the pale prospect
Of the river at dawn.

'Kavita', *Saat-ti Tarar Timir*

Loving You I Learn

Life, a drop of water
On the famed lotus leaf,
Seems so bright this morning.

Elusive droplet—
One moment it is there,
Next, it is gone.
Loving you, I learn this anew
Every time the night is over
On our lotus leaf.

You knew how for ages
I longed for you
And you, knowing it, turned yourself into a lotus leaf
For this incarnation.

Turning into the dew at night
You became the sound of it
Dropping into the silence
All night long.

Yet how am I to hold that droplet
On the leaf?

Longing to love forever,
I melted into the drop on the leaf;
I was lit up by your light
I gloried in your glories,
Made vows of everlasting love
In an ah! so transient life.

At last I learn the profound truth;
You and I are fated to meet
Only on the lotus leaf.

The sky is blue, the earth smiles,
Music comes from husking rice.
The lotus leaf trembles
Until the water evaporates.

                        'Tomake bhalobese', Agranthita Kavita

The Seagull

For a moment or two you and I
Are together in the sunlit sea.
Leaving the cradle of the Malabar Hills
Descends in a window the disant waves
Dance tarantellas of mystery;
White as snow their wings against the sky
Leap in joy like the waves to hail the earth;
Wipe out the songs of the vultures
On the crests of the hills;
Once more night of despair
Ends in reinvented dawn,
Life as green as grass.

Don't you know, seagull, that ages have passed
That rows of emperors are dead,
That fields of golden rice have turned to lead,
Leaving mankind tired, bereft of drive?
Wish, thought, dream, pain, future and the present
  that dins off-key music in our ears

I know, O you white bird, child of Malabar foam
You never look back,
You have no past, no memories;
You clutch no greying manuscripts to your breast.
Unlike earthly birds you do not face wintry nights filled with fog,
  mist, and pain
Not yours is the lonely morning
After the bloodletting of the night
And the resolves of the morning

Renewed by dreams
You do not dream.
Leaving the paths and the seas of the earth
You fly alone to an island within a magic mirror
To encounter a legendary beauty,
Her heart,
Gently rocked by ripples on the river of evening;
Her hair is as a shadow,
Her eyes dark as a forest of hijal trees;
Having once seen her,
All the world's lights have gone out
There, where golden honey has drained out isn't there any longer

There, where golden honey has drained out and the fly no more weaves its circuits
The smell of yellow leaves fills the heart of the still sparrow
The cloudy afternoon floats along
The golden kite longs for the beyond
Past the river with the terraced rice-fields
There, where there's none in the sky
Nor anyone on all the world's grass.

You know not that solitude;
Nor know that in the heart of the world's dust and blood
Still flows the grace of Kanchi and Vidisha
Like moving clusters of flies
Beauty still places its hand in the caves of dark desire.
That man's desperate desires, blue with effort
To grasp the rainbow
Dissolves like the short-lived daylight of autumn.

All this pristine knowledge is lost on you
In the flourish of your restless wings
Around the coral reefs
Your white wings glisten in sunlight

Alongside the foam-children
In a heliotrope sky.
Icy white wings shine in the sun
Ignorant of the world's thoughts and dreams.

Once upon a time you took birth amidst the reeds;
And, leaving sad climes,
In hordes descended on Arab seas
And China's gulfs
breaking out of the struggles with icy winds.

You will not know, never know,
The world's tales of rice, of the soft touch of its autumns
Or of the conch-shell-pale maidens,
the solitude on the faces of its lovers
Alive as dry grass;
With distant cackle they fly
Away in search of mild climes
Driven by the force of the ever-burning sun.

'Sindhu saras', *Mahaprithivi*

The Night

Turning the hydrant on
—Or perhaps it was always on anyway,
Being out of order—
The leper licks up water.
Midnight descends in hordes upon the city.
A motor car rushes past
Coughing like a moron
Restlessly sprinkling petrol.

—And I pass Phear's Lane—
Walking miles for no reason—
Gain Bentinck Street, stand leaning on a wall
Emerge in Terity Bazar dry as a peeled peanut;

The heat of drunken lamps
Caresses my cheek.
Kerosene, wood, lac and the smell of leather
Merge into the rattle of a dynamo
To keep life's bowstring taut.
Keep taut the earth's living and dead.

Once upon a time Moitreyi spoke;
Once Attila conquered;
Yet from the window above
In a voice all her own
A Jewish woman, half awake,
Sings to the world.
Our ancestors assemble to wonder
When is a song a song
And when metal, oil, or coal mine?

Smartly dressed Eurasian youths pass by;
Leaning on a pillar an old Negro laughs;
Gorilla-like, the old man cleans his pipe,
Finds the great night of the city
Oddly like the jungles of Libya,
But its animal denizens unique, too highly paid;
Indeed, he decides,
They wear clothes to cover their shame.

'Ratri', *Saat-ti Tarar Timir*

Within My Head

I move between light and dark
And feel within my head
A sense gathering force
That I cannot dismiss;
It's not a dream, not a breath of peaceful air
Nor love. It places its hand upon mine
Suddenly, making all action seem vain
Inane, empty.

Who has it in his power
To be simple?
Who can move, stop, think, speak
With candour, in this forever twilight?
Who knows for certain what is worth knowing?
Who ventures to know the feel of the body
The scent of water on the skin?
Who will plant the seedlings
And find joy in the harvest?
Body smeared with smell of mud
Who will with peasant soul
Embrace the earth?
Neither peace nor love or dream
But some other being
Hovers within the head.

I want to ignore him.
In my comings and goings,
I try to drive him away
To smash his skull to pieces
But like a living thing, relentlessly,
He keeps circling me.

I live amongst all, yet alone;
Am I the only one to be blinded by the light
Puzzled by the many ways open before me?

Take the ones who have taken birth
On earth, gave, given, will give birth through life
Aren't their hearts and minds
    the same as mine?
Why then am I alone?

Have I not lifted the plough like any peasant?
Carried buckets of water
Sickle in hand, gone into the fields?
Like fishermen
Have I not wallowed in the puddles
And wrapped my body in the smell of fish
And water-weeds and algae
The same as they?

All this I have tasted;
Like the wind has life flown;
Under the canopy of stars my mind has slept;
My boundless wishes I've fulfilled without let;
Yet one day I have left them behind.

I have known the love of woman,
Covered her with glory, neglect, scorn;
She has showered her love upon me
First drawn close, then pushed me aside in scorn.
One day I returned her hatred with love—
Love was then the language of my life
For whose sake I disregarded her neglect.
I forgot the stars whose conjunctions
Spelled impediment to my loves
Yet those loves were as dust on my way.

Within me there works
A sense—not a dream, not love.
I leave my gods behind
For recourse to my own heart.
And ask it why he whispers to himself
In endless eddies in the water?
He has no time for all else
No time for peace, for sleep
For lying alone,
Awake, in silence:
Find joy in the face of man, woman, child?

This sense,
This secret, endless wish
Living in the bosom of the deep—
He won't take the high road to nebulae
But cling to the earth?
Has he sworn he must
Look upon the face of man, woman and child,
Taking upon himself
All the deafness that can beset the ears
All the rottenness that can cling to overripe fruit,
Blighted vegetables, dessicated flesh—
And blossom in the human heart.

'Bodh', *Dhusar Pandulipi*

The Vultures

Across the skies of Asia, winging through the afternoon light
From one vast field to another the vultures fly,

Walk the silent meadows far from the tenements of man;
Where the firm silence of the earth
Stretches like another sky, there the vultures land softly
From the dense cloud—elephant guardians
Of the quarters of the sky, stricken by smoke,
Deflected from distant light, fallen on the fields
Dead but for a moment, climbing again the dark wide-winged
                                              palms,
Wafted from hill to hill, reaching open sea,
They watch the ship around gather in the dark into Bombay's port,

Circling some moaning tower beyond the pale of earthly birds
Their wings take them beyond an undefined death;

Is it the river of oblivion or the dim lagoon of life's severance
That moans in the deep . . . watches the hordes melt into the blue.

                                               'Sakun', *Dhusar Pandulipi*

Suchetana

Like an island far as the star of evening
Are you, Suchetana,
There, where among the forests of cinnamon trees
There is peace.

The world's blood and toil and glory
Are true; yet the last truth they are not.
Let Kolkata be the pride of heaven some day;
Yet shall my heart be yours.

I have striven, worn my feet roving.
Seeking to give man what belongs to him,
And I am weary roving in the burning sun of day.
Yet so striving to love man,

I see man, my own flesh and blood,
Strewn around dead, killed by my own hand.
The world is sick and in pain,
Yet we are its debtors, and shall remain.

I have seen the ships anchor in harbours
In the burning sun, laden with the crop of death;
Carcasses heaped of innumerable beings,
The wonder of dead flesh
Beaten into gold, silences us
As it did Buddha and Confucius.
Yet ceaselessly the gory world sounds its call
And beckons to us all.

This is the road to life, Suchetana,
The road of deliverance,
But after many centuries
And many labours of the great—
How bracing this sun-warmed breeze:
Life as good as this we shall build
With our weary, tireless hands,
But not yet; that day will come.

The good earth called me to be born
In human home, and I,
Knowing I should not, yet came.
The meaning of this I know now;
For with the tip of my finger
I have touched the stuff
Of the dew on the leaf at dawn.

What I saw is what will happen
And what will happen
Is what seems not destined to happen—
In the timeless dark the eternal sunrise.

'Suchetana', *Banalata Sen*

The Streets of Babylon

I do not know what faint whisper has made me walk
Through the streets of the city, alone, from one post to another.
I have seen the trams and buses ply with such faith,
Then enter, at the end of day, into the world of sleep.
All night long the gas lamps do their duty so well;
None errs; bricks and houses, windows and roofs
All close their eyes at last under the sky.
I have felt their peace in my bones, walking through
The dead streets of the night; seen them gathered
Round the top of the tower; it seems I have not seen
A simpler, more moving event. The starlit city, crowded with
towers;

The eye moves down and takes in the burning cigarette stub,
The wisp of hay pushed along by the wind.
I close my eyes and move to a side—the tree
Has shed many brown, faded leaves, and they have fled.
So in the stillness of night have I walked
Through the streets of Babylon and of Calcutta
Why? I know no more than I knew centuries before.

'Path hanta', Banalata Sen

The Corpse

Here, where the silvery moon lies wet in the forest of reeds
Where many mosquitoes have hopefully built their homes;

Where, wrapped up in themselves, and silent in desire,
The golden fish devour the blue mosquitoes;

Where, in this far corner of the world, the river lies
Deep and alone, painted in the colour of the silent fish;

And lying next to the field, in the midst of tall grass,
The river's water stares endlessly at the pale red cloud;

Or the darkness of the starlit sky
Looks like the head of a woman with a knot of blue hair.

The world has other rivers; but this river
Is the red cloud, the yellow moonlight carved up in patches;

All other light and all other darkness has ended here,
Only the red and blue fish and the cloud remain;

Here, forever, floats the corpse of Mrinalini Ghosal
Red and blue, silvery and silent.

'Shab', *Mahaprithivi*

The Cat

All through the day I keep meeting the cat;
In the shade of the tree, out in the sun,
Amidst the dense shade of the leaves.
After a spot of success with a few bones of fish
He lies hugging the skeletal-white earth
Wrapped up in himself like a swarm of bees.
And yet he scratches at the trunk of the gulmohar tree,
Walks behind the sun, stalking it.
One moment he is there;
The next, he has vanished.
I saw him in the autumn evening, stroking, with soft white paws,
The scarlet sun; then he gathered the darkness
Like little balls, grabbing each with a jab of his paws
And spread them all over the earth.

'Biral', *Mahaprithivi*

One Day Eight Years Ago

He had been taken to the morgue, they said.
The moon had set, the darkness had arisen
Last night, the fifth night of the moon, when he felt
A rush of affection for death.

Next to him lay his bride, his child;
Yet what ghost did he see in the moonlight
Beyond love, beyond hope? How come he awoke?
Had he not slept for long? Did he long to sleep?

Was this the sleep of his longing—
The sleep of the plague rat, foaming blood at the mouth,
Neck thrust into the dark crevice,
Never to wake again?

'Never to awake, never to know
The unbearable burden of knowing,
And knowing always, never'—
Said to him, after the moon had set,
A silence, creeping up to his window,
Like a camel's neck.

Yet the owl keeps awake, longs to live;
The aged frog begs for two moments
Warming to the hope of another dawn.

Around the defeating net I hear
The mosquito's desperate roar
Keeping in the dark a cloistered vigil
Belonging, with love, to life.

From the spittle, the blood and the excreta
The fly rises into the sunlight,
The golden sunlight gleaming with insect wings.

A pervasive life like a close-lying sky
Holds them all in its thrall;
The grasshopper struggles with the child's strangling hand;
And yet, when the moon had set, rope in hand
You departed in the dark for the banyan tree
(Not for man indeed the life of the insect).

Did not the branch of the banyan protest?
Did not the fireflies swarm the golden flowers?
Did not the doddering blind old owl declare—
'Time to catch a rat, now that the moon has set.'
Did not the owl whisper this wisdom in your ear?

This feel of life, the smell of ripe corn this autumn afternoon
You spurned, to be dead as the trampled rat
With the blood-smeared mouth, seeking refuge
From the agonies of your soul?

Listen yet to the tale of this dead.
No failures in love; life in matrimony
Left no yawning gaps;
The churning of time turned up
The right trace of honey in the everyday, in the mind;
A life unshaken ever by the fevers of the have-not.
Dead nevertheless.
Spreadeagled on the table, in the morgue.

We know, do we not,
That neither love nor the heart of woman
Or the touch of the child, the warmth of home

Suffice unto man; that beyond all glory
And achievement, there lies in our blood
That which drains us of all,
Empties us from within.
The morgue, we know, puts an end to it all.
Spreadeagled on the table, that is where you lie.
Yet every night I look at the decrepit owl
Back on the banyan tree and hear it say,
(And here it rolls an eye):
'Time to catch a rat, now that the moon has set.'

O grandpa, my grandpa profound!
I shall also, like you, stay and grow old!
The old moon I shall wash out with the ecliptical flood
And when the dark descends
Hand in hand the two of us shall raid and empty
The world of plenty.

'Aat bachhar ager ekdin', *Mahaprithivi*

The Windy Night

The night was windy last night—and full of stars.
The whole night the wind played on the net over my head
Sometimes swelling it like the monsoon-tossed sea
Sometimes tearing it away from the bed
And wafting it away towards the stars.

At times—half-awake—I felt
The net was no longer overhead
It was flying like a white balloon over the blue sea past the stars.

All the dead stars had come to life last night—
There was no room in the sky to hold them all
I saw the faces of all the beloved dead among the stars.
Stars shining in the dark like the dew-moist eyes of the
Love-laden kite upon the banyan tree;
The whole wide sky was glittering like a leopard-skin shawl
Flung across the shoulders of some Babylonian queen;
Such a marvellous night was last night.

Stars that had died many thousands of years ago
Peeped in through the window last night
Carrying with them each its own dead sky;
The damsels whom I had seen perish in Assyria, Egypt and Vidisha
Stood there, spear in hand, in rows across the misty edge of the
                                                                       sky.

To conquer death? To celebrate the victory of life?
To raise awesome monuments to love?

I feel torn, crushed, dazed by the torment of the night;

Under the ceaseless widespread wings of the sky
The earth was brushed away like a fly
And from the depths of the sky descended the wild winds
Screaming through my window
Like a thousand zebras in the flaming yellow steppes
Leaping to the roar of the lion.

My heart is filled with the smell of the green grass of the veld
Of the burning sun stretched across the endless fields
And with the hairy, wild, huge ecstasy of the darkness
Like the roar of the mating-mad lioness
And with the blue, tearing madness of living.

My heart tore itself from its moorings on earth
And flew like a swollen, drunken balloon across the blue sky
Like a distant star-mast flung across space,
Heady as an eagle.

'Hawar raat', *Mahaprithivi*

Wild Swans

The grey wings of the owl swing away towards the stars;
Across the marshland, beckoned by the moon
The wild swans fly across the marsh;
The rising sibilance of a myriad wings assail the ears;

Along the edge of the night their rapid wings,
Sounding like engines, fly, fly into the night
Leaving behind them an expanse full of stars,
The smell of swan bodies—and some swans of fancy.

Suddenly the face of Arunima Sanyal swims into view
Rising out of a dim past in forgotten villages.
Fly, fly in silence in this winter moonlight,
O you swans of fancy, keep flying after all the noises of the world
                                                                  have fled
Fly deep within the moonlit silence of the heart.

                                                    'Buno haans', *Mahaprithivi*

The Aeons, Like Fireflies

Amid the darkness of time
The aeons, like fireflies, dance.

The moonlight spreads itself upon the sands;
The shadows of tall deodars
Lie still; fallen columns of the lost kingdom,
Faded and dead, in silence frozen.
The world's noises have faded.
Our bodies are wrapped in the sleep of death;
There is a faint odour of the dead in the air.
A faint rustle and a voice asked:
'Remember?'
'Banalata Sen?' asked I.

                    'Hajaar bachhar shudhu khela karey', *Mahaprithivi*

Winter Night

On such nights does death creep into my heart.
The old owl sings of the fallen leaves and the dew;
Between the end of the town and the beginning of the country
Roars the lion—
The stricken lion of the dusty circus.
Through the depths of the winter night
The cuckoo sings too, all of a sudden,
Telling the world that spring was,
And will be, again.

But I have seen countless cuckoos grow old
Myself am a little like the aged bird.
The lion roars again
The stricken lion of the dusty circus,
Ageless, doped, blind, and plunged in darkness.
Seeking the remainders of life in the sea around,
In the living moss stuck to the tail of the dead fish
All is lost in the mist, in the endless water.
Never again
Never again
Shall the lion find the forest
The cuckoo's song
Like a broken machine shall disintegrate
And lose itself in bits and pieces
To the silent, magnetic mountain below.
O world hugging the river of oblivion,
Turn on your side and go to sleep again
For no surprise awaits you around the corner
None at all, at all, ever again.

'Sheetbastra', *Mahaprithivi*

Into These Ears

Gazing at the stars
Nursing the pain in their hearts
The young men poured out poetry, and departed.

The dumb beauties of the world half-heard their words
In ignorant awe
Yet, into the ears of these inert deaf golden images of brass
Alas, the young men poured countless immortal words;
Gazing at the stars
Nursing the pain in their hearts.

'Ihaderi kaane', *Mahaprithivi*

Nine Swans

I see nine swans in the water
Soft as the olive leaf, every morning.
Three times three makes nine by logic
But these become nine by some sheer magic.

The river is deep, fathomless
The light white cloud dips into it
And dives down and further down
And yet does not reach the end of time.

On all sides the tall grass spreads a soft bed
Still autumn waters have become the blue sky
The flock of swans has merged into the soft afternoon light
Far in the lap of some pale woman;
The colour of puffed rice flows from the basket—

Suddenly the river becomes a river
I remember the nine swans.

'Haans', *Mahaprithivi*

In the Likeness of the Sun

After continual crisis comes the danger
Failing to affect us
Turning into a matter of understanding—
And no more.
The river's water flows through the sand,
The sun flashes over it now and then;
The silvery bird flies out above the water.
Death and pity are as two crossed swords
That destroy and rebuild the town, the bridge, the human quarter;
The sky sharp as a blade lies above.

So it has been a long time—watched over by the sun and the wind.
Those that saw it all, loved it all
Time in its exigent wisdom has put up for sale,
And they have vanished.

Come then, let us to ourselves and to our own worlds
Determine to shine in total truth.
Is time marching towards a new dawn?
O quarters of the earth, somewhere I hear the bird,
Somewhere there is sunrise yet to be met.
Not only death—
But what is visible over the ocean of death
By advancing upon it we have seen,
Some of it we have forgotten, some remembered.
And even after obtaining our discharge
From the sand, the blood and the grime of the earth
Even in the darkness of the in-between
We have given the whore the slip
And to the lover taught deceit
All in cold blood, have we not?

The revolutionary turns to the gold,
The lover submerged in lifelong death,
Finds bliss in the caravan's delicate merchandise;
Where then lies, beyond our seeing, the affirmation of life?

We wait upon the silent hour;
Among the miles upon bewitched miles of ocean
Before moonrise fly the birds and so must we,
Forgetting the moon,

Fly, fly in this eternal moment before the light.
The waves behind have deceived us and gone past;
In front advances the benumbed endless ocean;
Fluttering with broken salt-wounded wings
Like traitors some have fallen along the dark lanes of the sea.
Death like this has been countless
And will be.

'Ending the death of individuals
We are all dead ourselves'—
With such death rooted in their hearts.
In dismissing history's wide-flung space,
All along the edges of the furthest-receded spirit of man
They arise again in the endless dark sunlit spree,
Of nineteen forty-three, forty-four, and eternity.

'Surjapratim', *Saat-ti Tarar Timir*

Epitaph

Here lies Sarojini; (I do not know
If she still lies here); she has lain here for long;
Then, perhaps, she has arisen and merged into the cloud
That is lit up where the darkness ends.

Went up there, did she, Sarojini,
Without a ladder, or the wings of a bird?
Or is she a mere parcel of the earth's geometry?
But that spectre says: No, I do not know.

A dry saffron light lingers in the sky
Like an invisible cat
On whose face sits an obstreperous smile
Of hollow cunning.

'Saptak', *Saat-ti Tarar Timir*

The Traveller

Aeons ago, it would seem,
In the limpid waters of some distant ocean
Life began.

Behind it lay the hieroglyphic fog,
Bereft of birth and death, of identity.
Forgetting slowly the language of that fog,
Falling in love unknowingly with some undefined being—
And drawn to the light, the sky, and the water
A new meaning grew, on the earth cradle.

So entwining in his heart
The black and white of death and life
Man has come on his journey to earth.
Amidst the inky skeletal dust, the blood strewn all round
Picking my way along the signposts of shiftless longing
I came to make known the sign of my birth in this dust—
To whom?
The earth? The sky? The sun that burns in the sky?
The speck of dust, the atom, the molecule, the shade, the rain. The
                                        droplet of water?
The city, the port, the state, the world of knowledge and ignorance?
The fog that hung over our birth
The fog that will remain entangled with our death
Bends now its darkness towards the ellipse of light;
The mind swims out in love to the blue expanse
Urging us on to the ageless dark ocean.

Yet every day
The sun brings with it

The day, the light, the way of life and of death
Whose meaning to eternal history
Remains unfathomed.

Towards this end man marches
Love and decay and pain marking his every step,
The river and the human heart, grey and forever flying,
Reach the end of night at dawn—the countless dawns of the eternal
story—
New suns, new birds, new signs in towns and habitations
With new travellers merge the travellers to the land of life;
In their hearts there is light and song and journey's rhythm—
The journey without end, perhaps given to man, in eternity.

'Jatri', *Sreshtha Kavita*

Anupam Tribedi

Anupam Tribedi's face fades in on this cold night,
Although he is no longer physically tumbling
Inside the belly of the rotund earth.
The silence of winter standing at the table
Brings his memory bustling back into the thoughts
Of the dead and the living; the books on the table
Bend the mind to all from Plato to Tagore
Who, after emptying their thoughts on us,
Sleep now under dewy blankets out in the cold.
Tribedi, having snuffed out his candle on earth,
Must be waking them from their slumber;
Bodhi and resurrection, tantra and cabala
Hegel and Marx had been pulling him along by the ear
In opposite directions, when,
Arms akimbo, brows knitted,
Suddenly he knew he liked love better than knowledge,
And a totem even better than love;
As the image of the camel—in a woman's heart—
Bent upon the conquest of mirage
She walks; the cream-coloured sari clings to her form.
Look closely and discover
How clever the readymade lady—surely from South Bengal?
The knot at sari's end hardly in focus,
Sweeping through Uttarpara and Bandel, Kashipur and Behala
Bearing the load of the Stalins, the Nehrus or some Block or Roy.
If past the three cubits of earth there be further sacrificial space,
It can't be love; or so thinking, Tribedi lost heart.
Ears pulled by equal dialectic we live
Between spirit and substance; Tribedi's was pulled too hard.

'Anupam Tribedi', *Sreshtha Kavita*

The Harvest Is Over

The harvest is long over.
Strewn over the fields lie
Straw, leaves, eggshells, sloughed snakeskins;
Amidst them, in the cold, sleep a few known faces.

One among them, one that one saw often,
And sinned against, playing games of the heart;
Wrapped in peace today
Lies under the grass and the grasshoppers
That envelope his thoughts and his enquiring mind
With darkness.

'Dhankata hoye gachhey', *Banalata Sen*

Rainy Night

In the heart of the deep dark rain
I am awakened, slowly,
By the rolling of the waves
In the Bay of Bengal
Hundreds of miles away.

The dark sky lies still
Holding the curves of the earth in its arms
Listening to the sounds of the sea.

At the distant lighted edge of the sky
I hear huge gates swinging open
And being closed again.

Heads resting on pillows they sleep
In order to awake tomorrow.
The faint lines of laughter and love
That lay etched deep into the moist, ancient rock
Stir slowly as they come to life.
From the depths of the unshaken earth they seek me out
And bring me out into the night.

The rolling of the bay comes to an abrupt stop;
Miles upon miles of earth lie still in silence.

A misty hand is laid on my shoulder
I hear a whisper say—
If I would touch those gates swinging open and closing again,
I could, on a night like this.

I raise my eyes
And like a grey cloud
Enter through the double doors of darkness
Into a cavernous mouth that devours me.

'Shravan raat', *Mahaprithivi*

The Smell of Far Worlds

Smells from far ends of the earth
Invade my Bengali mind tonight.

If one day death asks me
To lie down below unfamiliar grass
On some unknown planet,
That grass will fill my breath
With the scent of aniseed, like Bengal's very own;
As a young mother's breast melts into milk
In any country, clime,
Under the light of the furthest star
All ways are laden with peace of this kind
Of grass, eyes, soft hands, breasts.

Somewhere death will come to me,
Cover me with the gentle fragrance of grass
At dawn, or at night;
Or a bird at mid-afternoon
Will take me to its bosom,
Cover me like grass;
The night sky will blossom into blue stars—
I don't know if the same stars shine in Bengal's skies
I know in their hearts there is peace
And in the body of the sky
They are as eyes, arms, breasts, grass.

'Dur prithivir gandhey', *Rupasi Bangla*

What Else, Before Death?

We who have walked the fields of hay in the autumn twilight
Seen the dim women at the river sprinkling the flowers of fog;
Women of the dim past, of distant villages;
We who have seen the trees filled with fireflies,
Seen the unavaricious moon stand at the top of the fields without
crop;

We who have loved the long, dark nights of winter,
Heard, upon the hay, in the enchanted night, the flutter of wings;

Smelled out the old owl and lost him again in the dark;
Felt the glory of the winter night
Filled with the rapture of wings across fields upon fields,
Heard the crane on the boughs of the ancient tree—
We who have delved these secret mysteries of life;

We who have seen the wild duck escape the hunter's aim
And fly to the end of the earth in the pale blue moonlight,
We who have placed our hands on sheaves of corn
And, like the evening crow, wound our way home full of longing;
Smelled the child's mouth, the grass, the sun, the bird, the star, the
sky—
We who have seen their marks on the cycle of the year;

Seen the green leaf turn yellow in the autumn night
The light and the bird play at the tree-framed window,
The rat in the winter night white with the flour,
Known the moist smell of the rice
Carried by the waves into the eyes of the solitary fish.

Across the pond the swan in the dark touched by the wand of
sleep,
Wafted away from all by the touch of some soft maidenly hand;

Clouds like minarets call the golden kite to their windows
Under the cane-creeper blue lies the sparrow's egg,
The river bathes its bank with the smell of soft-lapping water,
The shadow of the thatched roof is etched in the moonlit yard;
On the salt white slope descends the thick mist of tense longing;
The air is laden with the odour of crickets in the fields;

We who have seen the red fruits lying under the enraptured tree
The crowding fields watching their reflections in the river,
The blue skies seeking the depths of deeper blue,
Eyes cast their soft shadow across the paths of the earth;
We who have seen the evening descend down the row of betel-
nut trees

And the morning arrive easy and fresh as a sheaf of corn;
We who have known how the daughter of the earth
At the end of days, months and seasons,
Comes in the dark whispering of rivers; we who have known
That behind the fields and the paths and the steps to the tank
Shines another light, pale in the mellow afternoon,
Beyond the seeing of eyes, the unflickering light
There, where the lovely maidens of the world glide into bodies of
incense;
What else need we know before death? Do we not know
How at the edge of each red desire rises like a wall
The grey face of death? The dreams and the gold of the earth
Reach a tranquil equilibrium, ending a magic need.
What else need we know?
Have we not heard the cries of birds upon the dying sun?
Have we not seen the crow fly across the mist?

'Mrityur aage', *Dhusar Pandulipi*

I Will Leave It All

I will leave it all and turn into a tree
Standing against that red afternoon cloud.
I will peel off my human skin
And rub on my body
The scent of the tree's bark.
And in the falling light
I will encounter the flying bat.

The pale country path gets paler,
Leaning against the mountain's breast.
I will walk down that path;
And the wonder on the face of that mountain
I will wrap around me.

'Ami sab chhere diye', Agranthita Kavita

Starlight

Time and again, I shift my gaze from the star
To the field below.

It seems the scent of rice fields
Has been wiped out of life;
Sleepy are the fields, tired bearing the weight
Of even the stray bundles of remaining hay;
The stars awaken them with their light,
Whispering: 'Asleep, are you?'

The evening sky is crowded with stars;
I lie on grass that bears the shadows of spring.

It is time for death to arrive—
Blades of this grass will cling to my body,
The stars gathered above will stay close to me forever.

Someone sneezes—is it Hamid's blinkered old horse?
After the day's weary pulls
It blandly chews on a pile of moonlit grass
Without a care in the world.

Why then do I seek death?
'Why then do you seek death'—echoes a bantering sky.

Here, where fruits of coniferous trees
Spread themselves thick upon the grass,
Where the grasshopper has ended his day and left for home,
I lie, and ask of the star:

Tell me, evening star,
Which way should I go,
To escape from enterprise, enthusiasm,
dreams, thoughts,—
How shall I ever find peace?

'Go to your own place,'
Says the star with a sly smile,
'Or keep lying on the grass, loving my beauty,
Or stare at that bullock cart disappearing into the evening
Carrying its load of golden hay—
On the ground lies a snake's sloughed skin,
A stream sounds in the dark—
Quietly the cart goes, spreading peace;
Death does not touch its thoughts—
Though countless princes, potentates, behemoths
Have perished before it.'

'Niralok', *Mahaprithivi*

Three Stray Stanzas

Clouds in the sky have shed droplets of rain
Caking up the dust,
Suddenly sprinkling the smell of wet earth.
The train pulls out of the station;
Black rolls of smoke push out of the engine
And, jumping like bats, climb on to the moon,

A half-hour has passed.
A brougham and a hackney carriage
Have each gone their separate ways.
Now who comes there?
Are those the gig lamps on the Englishman's landau?
There is no sound from anywhere.
The wind has left the casuarinas alone.

I murmur your name—
But where are you at this moment, I wonder
—The scent of wet earth, the grass, the fallen leaves,
The dahlias, the kaminis—
No bird awakes alone like me;
Alone and helpless I take your name—
Where are you? Does anyone know?

'Stanza tinek', Agranthita Kavita

To You

I had thought I could assume, without caveat,
That in the mindless ocean of neutrons and electrons
And by their magic
You became woman
And I, by the same mathematics, your lover.

In the falling light of this winter afternoon
Farmers are taking the last of the harvest home;
Nature has watered the rivers;
Yet when blood spurts, it envelops all.

The century rolls; men and women move from the void to greater
                                                  voids,
from darkness into the further dark;
Other than this there is no truth
No one has other recourse.

Yet within this there is
More profound helplessness;
No man knows beyond man
And the everlasting shadow of man.
No sound of his will reach the deepest of the blue;

All is in order though;
From primordial slime you descend
Through blood, darkness and dishonour
Without revealing a shred of the context
That you carry in the dimple on your chin.

'Tomakay', Agranthita Kavita

Mortal Swans

Mortal swans have disappeared from here.
So have birds' nests from the trees.
Here the earth no longer exists, nor creation;

Only you and I lie.
And, against the night sky,
Stands the eternal tree.

'Maranshil haans', Agranthita Kavita

Death at the Turn of the Century

One disconnected day we were born
And now we die on a day more fevered.
Far and near, shadows on high and low walls
Instil fear in us which, when ruminated upon,
Leads from knowledge to sorrow
Or, having taken leave of knowledge
Hides behind the crystal door
Alone in the icy lake of assurance
Waiting for thigh to be broken by heroic hand;
Where hell fails to bring death and heaven compassion
And on earth sages spread tired disbelief in that dispensation.*

'Ei shatabdir sandhitay mrityu', Agranthita Kavita

---

* Translator's note: The reference here is obviously to an episode in the Indian epic, the Mahabharata, in which the warrior, Duryodhana, lies in the lake and is killed by Bhima by an unfair blow below the belt. The official view, sometimes questioned by moralists favouring the individual conscience, is that Duryodhana, being felled by unfair means, goes to heaven.